DEAR

Dawn Marie

DEAR. Copyright © 2020. DAWN MARIE. All Rights Reserved.

Printed in the United States of America.

No portion of this book may be reproduced, stored in a retrieval system, or transmitted in any form or by any means, except for brief quotations in printed reviews, without the prior written permission of Dawn Marie and HCP Book Publishing.

www.hcpbookpublishing.com

Book Cover Design by Keifer Simpson

ISBN: 978-1-949343-68-7 (paperback)

978-1-949343-69-4 (hardback)

This book is dedicated to women all over the world. May you always know how beautiful and amazing you are.

Dawn Marie

TABLE OF CONTENTS

Introduction 7
Dear Formerself: Chapter 1 10
Dear Formerself: Chapter 2 20
Journal Notes 30
Dear Formerself: Chapter 3 33
Learning To Forgive 43
Journal Notes 47
Dear Her 50
The Power Of Letting Go 61
Dear Him 63
Journal Notes 71
Dawn Marie 74

INTRODUCTION

I sat quietly in the meeting as he explained himself to the Bishop why he wanted to marry me. On one hand, I felt all these meetings were a sign to run. On the other hand, I kept reminding myself that he asked me to marry him. So, what if they do not think I am good enough? I am not marrying them, right? I could have been wrong.

I was alone in another meeting. This time I was told: "We will take care of the child, just get out of his life!" You probably already put the pieces together. Yes, I was pregnant and unmarried. To top it off, I already had a child out of wedlock. If you did not know, you too would probably think all the names I was referred to were very fitting.

Well, despite all the meetings and phone calls I received to get out of his life and to leave him alone, we got married. I was in love and I felt if he could still choose to marry me, despite all the hatred towards me, despite all the phone calls and threats, he must really love me too. So, on June 24, 2004 we said "I Do" in a small ceremony on the beach.

The week following the wedding was tense and quiet. Though we were happy and now dealing with the fact that we have a child on the way, he was saddened that they were not talking to him because of his decision to marry me. I started carrying his pain and when I should be gaining weight with the pregnancy, I was losing weight from the stress of his pain.

My doctor reminded me that I must stay calm for the baby's sake, so I decided to shift my focus and just love him and my unborn child more. But there was always something to break that silence. From other women sending me emails that he should have married them and not me, to comments about how lucky I am that he "took me up with a child." The sad thing is, the character that was formed and depicted about me was so far from the truth of who I am. I chose then not to fight this battle, and I did nothing.

I filled my life with work, my daughter, my niece and the baby on the way. Through all that was happening, I told no one in my family. I did not want to worry them and, furthermore, I felt terrible that all this was happening in the church with people serving God. Talk about being between a rock and a hard place! I finally understood what that statement meant.

The chapters you will read in this book is not a form of getting back or ruining anyone's life. God knows if all my sins were to flash on a screen, I would run and hide. However, in this book, I am simply just sharing my story with the hope that my openness will bring healing to another person that may be experiencing similar pain. I have spoken to many women over the years and recognized that so many are suffering in silence. My encouragement is that you talk to someone about it. There are spaces in this book allotted for you to write your own story, your own thoughts.

DEAR FORMERSELF
CHAPTER 1

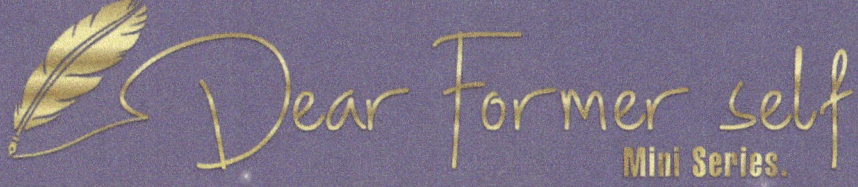

Dear Former Self
Mini Series.

Dear former Self:

Today I saw a woman. She was beautiful and dressed so well! And I thought of you and how beautiful you are, through all the pain, though it broke you, you remained so beautiful and **I'm proud of you.**

Inhale. Exhale. Express. Write freely here

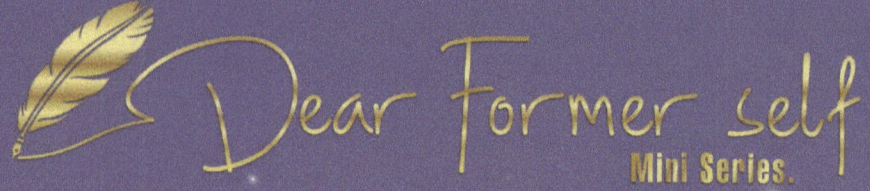

Dear Former self
Mini Series.

Dear Former Self:

I want to apologize to you for not treating you better. I should have not allowed them to call you names, especially not "prostitute"! I should have stood up for you more and protected you more. **I am sorry.**

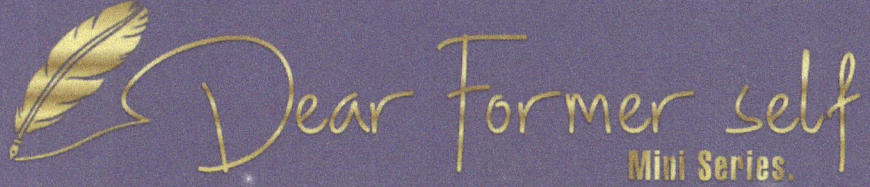

Dear Former Self:

I want to apologize to you for the verbal abuse...you know, like how "you gained weight after the babies and not attractive anymore", even though you were still a size 4.
I should have done something.
I am sorry.

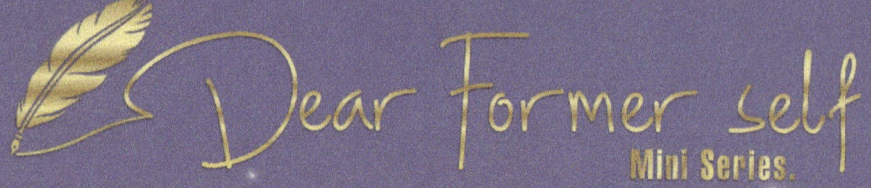

Dear Former Self:

I want to apologize to you for telling you not to leave when the affairs started before your first wedding anniversary. And after the second....and the others.... I kept telling you that God will fix it, just give it time. **I am sorry.**

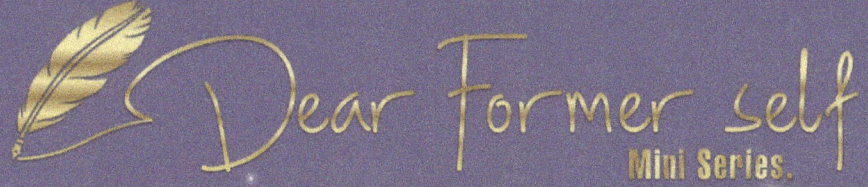

Dear Former Self:

I want to apologize to you for telling you to stay even when he brought her in your house, your bedroom and your bathroom.
I'm not sure what I was thinking.
I am sorry.

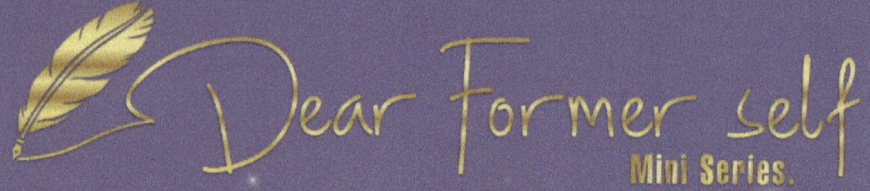

Dear Former Self:

I want to apologize to you for telling you to give him another chance even when he told you she is not dirty rags and he is not leaving her. I am sorry. **I am so sorry.**

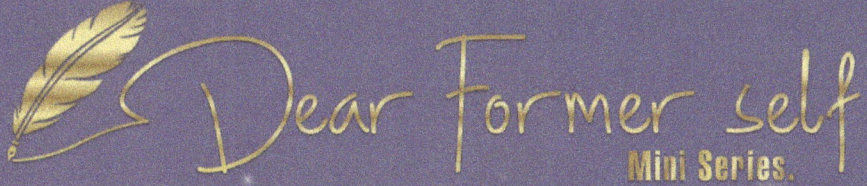

Dear Former Self:

I want to apologize for teaching you how to cover the pain with makeup and color correct the wounds of your heart. I should have taught you skincare instead! **I am sorry.**

Dear Former Self: Mini Series.

Dear Former Self:

I am sorry and I will keep apologizing to you until you are **whole!**

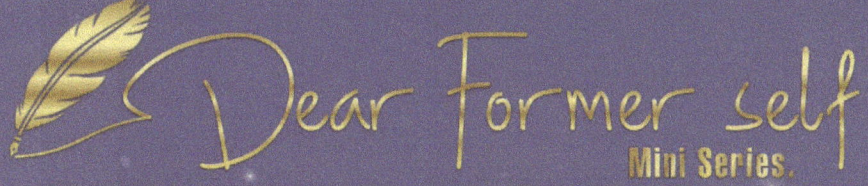

Dear Former Self:

Someone asked me "how do you forgive". With a smile on my face I started telling her that un-forgiveness is like drinking poison expecting the other person to die! Just let it go.
The sooner you forgive, the sooner your own healing comes. Girl, today I admire you for forgiving those who wronged you.

You are a true champion.

DEAR FORMERSELF
CHAPTER 2

Chapter 2

Dear Former Self:

I want to apologize to you for telling you that you are being too strong and it's not ladylike. The truth is, I only wanted you to take pieces off your crown so he could feel better about himself!
I am sorry.

Dear Former Self
Mini Series.
Chapter 2

Dear Former Self:

I've watched you lost yourself over the years. You stopped performing and achieving. I've watched you lost your zest for life, painting on your smile as you paint on your makeup each day. I've watched you screamed in a room packed with people yet no one heard your screams!
I am so sorry.

Chapter 2

Dear Former Self:

I remember seeing them together, over and over. I remember how uncomfortable it felt and when you confronted him he told you how insecure and jealous you were. Sigh. As always, he just had to find a way to turn the blame on you. You did well. Do you hear me? You did very, very well. **I am proud of you.**

Dear Former self
Mini Series.
Chapter 2

Dear Former Self:

He was supposed to love you. I know it hurts. You gave it your all. Dry your tears, you will be ok. Yes, love was supposed to be wonderful to you; and it was. It's in the eyes of your sons. Put a smile on and push your shoulders back. Girl, you are loved.

Dear Former Self
Mini Series.
Chapter 2

Dear Former Self:

"You're just too classy!"
Girl, you remember that?
Like really? When you were envied by so many others, you were being told you are too classy. I had a good laugh today. What decent man doesn't want a classy girl? You were just too much of a woman, that's all. Honey, **go out and be classy!**

Dear Former Self
Mini Series.
Chapter 2

Dear Former Self:

I did not realize that everything he is, was showing you who you are. You needed him. He was necessary in your life. I know it's hard to believe, but God has kept you. Purpose will be fulfilled. Lives will be transformed because of your story.

The pain was Purposed.

Dear Former Self: Mini Series.
Chapter 2

Dear Former Self:

I know it was hard waiting and going through the pain. But you know what, grapes don't become wine as soon as they are picked from the branches. They have to wait to ferment into quality wine. God only had you waiting because he is creating greatness in you!
Be strong.

Dear Former Self
Mini Series.

Chapter 2

Dear Former Self:

I want to apologize to you. I am sorry i allowed you to be mistreated. I thought about the breakfast meeting. The room was filled with people and she came over and stood in front of you, with her back facing you while she talked with him. No hello, no conversation, just totally ignored you and you were his wife! Why didn't I say something?
I am truly sorry.

Chapter 2

Dear Former Self:

I was thinking today about that time you got out of the shower and smiled with him. Instead of reciprocity, he pointed out all the flaws on your body and told you that you needed to get in the gym! Sigh. I felt the pain that cut through you that morning. I felt your self-esteem fell to the ground. And I stood there and did nothing! **I am so very sorry.**

JOURNAL NOTES

DEAR FORMERSELF
CHAPTER 3

Dear Former self
Mini Series.
Chapter 3

Dear Former Self:

Why do so many persons hurt you! I know you are loving and kind, but I feel everyone just abuse your kindness. Hang tight. **Better days are ahead.**

Chapter 3

Dear Former Self:

I feared for you some nights. When the panic attacks started and you had to take pills to sleep at nights, I really feared for you. One night you told him how scared you were and he asked **"why are you so afraid of death? Everyone has to die".** But all you wanted was for him to hold you and tell you everything was gonna be ok! You held your chest as though you were grasping for breath and replied, "and what will happen to my children then!"

Dear Former Self
Mini Series.
Chapter 3

Dear Former Self:

It was a **Thursday morning** and you were on bed rest from panic attacks and over exhaustion. The doctor told him it was either your health or the job! Funny that week he was so quiet and when you enquired he was upset that there was no intimacy those days you were in bed.
He went on to remind you that being on bed rest did not stop you from using the bathroom, ...read between the lines. I am really sorry honey. You should have packed your things then!

Dear Former Self
Mini Series.
Chapter 3

Dear Former Self:

You kept dreaming about a dark skinned girl. She appeared in your dreams several times. Couldn't really see her face, but her structure was so clear. Finally after you talked about it for weeks he confessed that there was another. The worst thing was they are people you knew and people who knew you! I wish I could have spared you the pain. **I am really sorry.**

Dear Former Self
Mini Series.
Chapter 3

Dear Former Self:

I am thinking about the day you took all the kids out of school, took them to the playground at the mall and turned your phone off. What was going through your mind? You kept staring at them as if you were telling them of your greatest pain without any words. **You were so lost and alone and not even the children's presence that once healed every pain, could heal the pain you were now feeling. I am sorry.**

Dear Former self
Mini Series.
Chapter 3

Dear Former Self:

Many will have **questions, maybe even ridicule.** But you listen to me, don't you quit sharing! You have been liberating many others and that was the purpose for your suffering. You are walking in #purpose. Keep walking.

Don't you Quit.

Dear Former Self
Mini Series.
Chapter 3

Dear Former Self:

That day your daughter addressed you as "Legend". OMG. I saw you giggled like a little girl. I am proud of you. In the midst of all you've endured,

you are indeed a Legend!

Dear Former Self
Mini Series.
Chapter 3

Dear Former Self:

When you speak everyone becomes quiet. It's a kind of silence that says "we want to hear what you have to say". Listen girl, you have fire inside of you.

Let nothing quench that.

LEARNING TO FORGIVE

"**D**awn, sex did happen," he told me. Luckily, I was already sitting on the toilet seat because I felt like everything in my stomach was going to come out. I remembered the evening so vividly. It was a Wednesday evening and we just got home from church. He was the speaker and his message was entitled: "The Truth, The Whole Truth and Nothing but the Truth." I got up quickly, got my car keys and drove off.

I had no particular destination; I just had to get out of the house. My heart was beating so fast I thought I was having a heart attack. I kept driving, not even watching where I was going. After about one hour on the road, I had no idea where I was. I pulled over by the side of the road and wept. I was not sure if I was crying about his confession or if I was crying about how he kept telling me that I was jealous and insecure every time I asked him about his relationship with her. I felt used, betrayed, unloved and I wanted to die.

The reality that my children were home suddenly hit me. A strong desire to live overcame me so I dried my tears, turned on my GPS, plugged in my address and went home. I kept asking God what to do. My sister lived in the same house with me. Do I tell her? Do I tell anyone? Do I stay? He gave me no answer. I went back home, checked on my children and went to bed.

The next day I managed to find the strength to take the children to school and go to work. I played the marriage vows over and over in my head all my way to work.

> "I, ___, take thee, ___, to be my wedded husband/wife, to have and to hold, from this day forward, for better, for worse, for richer, for poorer, in sickness and in health, to love and to cherish, till death do us part, according to God's holy ordinance; and thereto I pledge thee my faith [or] pledge myself to you."

Was this the "worse" that the vows spoke of? Am I supposed to forgive? But how? Honestly, I was a robot at work that day. Emotions had left me, and I became emotionless. My zest for life was suddenly zapped away from me. How do I forgive this?

The days following were quiet. I had so many questions in my head. Was I not good to him? How do I face her? Do I continue working with her? Am I going to be asked questions if I quit? My heart became weakened for many days and I became physically sick. My doctor suggested a series of test, including a pregnancy test based on my complains. As if God was punishing me for something, alas, I was pregnant again in the midst of all this. Every thought of leaving him left my heart. Who would want me divorced with two children and pregnant?

I started a study on forgiveness. After all, it now seemed like the best thing to do. I read many Scriptures and many books and quotes. The one that got me the most was "unforgiveness is like drinking poison and expecting the other person to die." That hit home. I did not want to die. I wanted to live and take care of my children. So, I wrote both a letter, telling them I forgive them.

Forgiveness is the fragrance that the violet sheds on the heel that has crushed it.

Mark Twain

What then is forgiveness? Forgiveness is the intentional and voluntary process by which a victim undergoes a change in feelings and attitude regarding an offense and lets go of the negative emotions, for example, resentment and vengeance (however justified it might be), and with an increased ability to wish the offender well.

> *Ephesians 4:31-32: Let all bitterness, wrath, anger, clamor, and evil speaking be put away from you, with all malice. And be kind to one*

another, tenderhearted, forgiving one another, even as God in Christ forgave you. (NKJV).

Matthew 6:14-15: For if you forgive men their trespasses, your heavenly Father will also forgive you. But if you do not forgive men their trespasses, neither will your Father forgive your trespasses. (NKJV).

What can I say but that learning to forgive has liberated me.

JOURNAL NOTES

DEAR HER

DEAR HER

Woman to Woman if you've even been in love!

Dear Her,

YOU WERE THE DARK-SKINNED GIRL IN MY DREAMS. I thought this can't be real. He said you were his friend. We did not even celebrate our **FIRST WEDDING ANNIVERSARY!** But then I found out he told you I was his friend! I can only imagine how much it would have hurt you knowing we were now married.
I am sorry.

DEAR HER

Woman to Woman if you've even been in love!

Dear Her,

One day I called and he said he was on an office trip. I heard your voice In the background. I couldn't understand why a trip so close to home needed a hotel room. **WHAT COULD I HAVE DONE FROM THOUSANDS OF MILES AWAY? SIGH.** It was you and him in a hotel room and we were only married for a few months.

DEAR HER

Woman to Woman if you've even been in love!

Dear Her,

I read your apology email. I read it several times actually. And I was convinced it was over. Well, physically it was, but emotionally it never ended. If what you both shared in your messages were true, then I was a fool for forgiving him and giving him a second chance. **DID HE LOVED YOU BUT MARRY ME?**

DEAR HER

Woman to Woman if you've even been in love!

Dear Her,

I've wondered about love and marriage and commitment. I didn't see this coming. **I THOUGHT I WAS GOOD TO HIM.**

DEAR HER

Woman to Woman if you've even been in love!

Dear Her,

So now you are a wife and a mother. **I PRAY YOU NEVER EXPERIENCE THE PAIN I'VE ENDURED.** I hope you are happy now.

DEAR HER

Woman to Woman if you've even been in love!

Dear Her,

I couldn't help but wonder if you were hurting too. You seemed so in love, I'm assuming. I saw the undeniable look of affection in your eyes each time you saw him. But every time I mentioned it, he would tell me I'm being insecure! **I'M SORRY THAT HE BROKE YOUR HEART TOO.**

DEAR HER

Woman to Woman if you've even been in love!

Dear Her,

We shared the same space. I wanted to hate you, so badly. But there was such innocence in you, my heart would not let me. I am just thinking how hard this was for you. Sigh. If you loved him as much as I loved him then I know your pain was just as real.

I AM SORRY.

DEAR HER

Woman to Woman if you've even been in love!

Dear Her,

I cannot describe the pain you have caused me. But there are days I asked myself, **"DID SHE REALLY CAUSE ME PAIN OR DID HE?"** You knew me, you knew my children, you befriended them, you betrayed me. And with all that, I cannot help but say **I AM SORRY FOR YOUR PAIN.**

DEAR HER

Woman to Woman if you've even been in love!

Dear Her,

I REMEMBER SEEING THE EMAILS BETWEEN THE TWO OF YOU. Your expression of love and adoration for him cut through me like a knife. Will I ever survive this? I did, and now **I CAN SAY I AM SORRY BECAUSE YOU TOO LOST YOUR LOVE!**

DEAR HER

Woman to Woman if you've even been in love!

Dear Her,

I remember confronting you. Every question I asked you was so properly fixed and aligned to his answers. It was obvious you both planned your answers. I left that day thinking "Jesus needed Judas to betray Him so purpose could be fulfilled". That day I forgave you and set you free. You played your role in my life. **THANK YOU AND I AM SORRY YOU WERE HURT.**

THE POWER OF LETTING GO

The night was chilly. I wrapped a blanket around me as I sat awake in the bed, frightened by another dream I just had. Expressing myself the way I know best, I got up and wrote this poem. The next morning, I told him the dream I have been having and once again I was reliving the pain I thought I forgave. It was not a mere dream, but there was yet another.

I chose to forgive and let go, but now I started having dreams.

Seriously God! What else? The consistency of this one is overwhelming.

Are there others or is my mind playing tricks on me?

There was no clear vision of her but her silhouette consumed my mind: dark-skinned, short, beautiful –

God are you trying to tell me something?

I guess you were, because then the other confession came.

Seriously, how do I go on?

Let it go: but how?

Okay, Okay I hear You.

Quotes that helped me to let go:

The truth is, unless you let go, unless you forgive yourself, unless you forgive the situation, unless you realize that the situation is over, you cannot move forward.

Steve Maraboli

If you want to fly in the sky, you need to leave the earth. If you want to move forward, you need to let go of the past that drags you down.

Amit Ray

In the process of letting go, you will lose many things from the past, but you will find yourself.

Deepak Chopra

The only thing a person can ever really do is keep moving forward. Take that big leap forward without hesitation, without once looking back. Simply forget the past and forge toward the future.

Alyson Noel

DEAR HIM

DEAR HIM
When a Woman **Loves!**

Dear Him,

There is so much I could say. But I'm choosing to close this chapter of my life with only good things: I have loved you more than love itself. I forgive you for all the pain you have caused me. I hope you will forgive me too. I'm sure I have done my share of pain. You have played your role in my life. **Thank you.**

DEAR HIM
When a Woman Loves!

Dear Him,

One day you came to pick me up. You had on a crisp white shirt and a pair of blue jeans. I honestly didn't think my heart would calm down. Not even Usain could run that fast. Lol. Your entire face smiled when you saw me and I've never felt so special.

I knew that day I was in love!

DEAR HIM
When a Woman **Loves!**

Dear Him,

OMG, we are Married! I can still feel the butterflies in my stomach thinking about it. You were to say your vows instead you sang the song "Now and Forever". Smiley face here! I wanted the wedding to end right there so I could spend the evening with you. But even with all that love, and happiness, **you were so saddened that your parents never came.**

DEAR HIM
When a Woman Loves!

Dear Him,

Saturdays became my safe haven. No matter how rough or frustrated my week was, there was nothing that Saturdays with you and Moulin Rouge wouldn't solve. I should know every scene from that movie by now. I still have the playlist on my phone. Some memories are worth keeping. Smiles.

DEAR HIM
When a Woman **Loves!**

Dear Him,

One day we visited a church. You kept saying that the keyboard sounded off. You would not listen to me telling you to forget about the keyboard and pay attention to the worship. Instead after church, you asked the pastor if you could take a look inside the keyboard. Well, you were right. There was a dead rat inside the keyboard! I was just amazed at how keen you were to the sounds of music! **I pray that you start honing your gifts.**

DEAR HIM
When a Woman Loves!

Dear Him,

Our first born always open the car door for me whether I'm driving or getting in a taxi. I know where he gets that from, and I just smile. Thank you for the little things. **#heopensthecardoor**

Dear Him,

I've always told you that I see greatness inside of you. Funny you would always tell me you do not see that person. We make decisions based on how we value ourselves. We are all in need of God's Grace and His Forgiveness. Your past does not have to dictate your future. **YOU HAVE GREATNESS IN YOU.**

JOURNAL NOTES

DAWN MARIE

Dawn Marie Lindo is a Minister of Religion, Businesswoman, Motivational Speaker and Makeup-Artist. Dawn is the founder and CEO of the D'Marie Institute Limited since October 2009. Leveraging her experience and training at top international cosmetics houses such as Estee Lauder, Mac and Clinique, Dawn Lindo ensured that the D'Marie Institute earned its place as Jamaica's best institution of its kind, dedicated to offering exceptional skills training, exquisite makeup products and cutting edge information for students and clients to guide their choices about their individual beauty and personal care needs.

D'MARIE'S stunning list of awards includes being the winner of the City & Guilds Medal for Excellence Award 2014; Winner of the MUA Essential Award for Best Makeup School and Best in Makeup Artistry 2014; the JMUA Makeup Guru Award 2016 and 2018 and recently nominated for the BID Quality Award in Paris, France. The institution is registered with the Ministry of Education and is accredited by City & Guilds of London.

Lindo is among the leading lights in the arena of corporate customer service, grooming and makeup training, and she has shared her real-world experiences working on runway shows, pageants, a slew of corporate events and top notch music videos.

Her motivational talks and dynamic customer service presentations have made her central to the arsenal of leading companies looking to hone the leadership skills of their staff over the course of a stellar 22-year career.

Trained in the United States, Britain and Jamaica, Dawn Lindo received an Associate degree from Bergen Community College, after which she continued to complete a Masters degree in Counseling Psychology and is highly trained as an innovative beauty specialist, makeup artist, educator, lecturer and businesswoman.

She has worked as Instructor of Makeup Artistry and Beauty Therapy at the College of Beauty Services in Kingston, Jamaica and as a Department Manager for Nordstrom and Dillard's in the USA.

Her training, education and professional experience, combined with her winning personality, led to her copping major accolades including the Nordstrom Team Titan Award, the Warwick Development Centre Certificate of Achievement, the New Jersey Harold Profile, Pillar of Strength Award, Annual Makeup Profiles in the Jamaica Observer, and numerous pageant awards, including Caribbean Fashion Week, Caribbean Model Search, Miss

Universe Jamaica, as well as management, civic and professional awards locally and globally.

Dawn's purpose in life is to educate and motivate.

IG: @officialdawnmarie

FB: Offical Dawn Marie

Gmail: dawnmarieofficial@gmail.com